To the Balmer family for opening your hearts and setting a place
at the table with the invitation of love.
To my ever-present loving family, for your love and encouragement.
To my heavenly Father for adopting me into your family.

LUCY'S ADOPTION SONG
Copyright ©2025 Sandee Macgregor
Illustrated by Kim Sponaugle

ISBN: 978-1-998815-29-6 Soft Cover
ISBN: 978-1-998815-31-9 Hard Cover
ISBN: 978-1-998815-30-2 Ebook

Published by Castle Quay Books, Burlington, Ontario
Tel: (416) 573-3249 | E-mail: info@castlequaybooks.com | www.castlequaybooks.com

Edited by Marina Hofman Willard

All rights reserved. This book or parts thereof may not be reproduced in any form without prior written permission of the publishers.

This is a work of fiction. Names, characters, businesses, places, events and incidents are either the products of the author's imagination or used in a fictitious manner. Any resemblance to actual persons, living or dead, or actual events is purely coincidental.

Scripture quotations are taken from the The ESV® Bible (The Holy Bible, English Standard Version®). ESV® Text Edition: 2016. Copyright © 2001 by Crossway, a publishing ministry of Good News Publishers. The ESV® text has been reproduced in cooperation with and by permission of Good News Publishers. All rights reserved.

**Cataloguing in Publication information can be obtained through Library and Archives Canada.**
Title: Lucy's adoption song / written by Sandee Macgregor ; illustrated by Kim Sponaugle.
Names: Macgregor, Sandee, author | Sponaugle, Kim, illustrator
Identifiers: Canadiana (print) 2025020553X | Canadiana (ebook) 20250205548 | ISBN 9781998815319
   (hardcover) | ISBN 9781998815296 (softcover) | ISBN 9781998815302 (EPUB)
Subjects: LCGFT: Picture books. | LCGFT: Fiction.
Classification: LCC PS8625.G7439 L83 2025 | DDC jC813/.6—dc23

# Foreword

As a couple, it's been our desire to seek the Lord's will and hold nothing back that the Lord might desire of us. That means all of our time and love resources are available for his use. This certainly applied to raising children and adopting them.

It's heartbreaking for us to consider that there are children who grow up without loving parents and the daily provisions that they need. How could we say no to giving back when God has given us so much?

Yes, we have made sacrifices along the way, but he has blessed us abundantly. Each of our children has blessed us in different ways. It's a thrill and honor to have people in our lives who call us Mom and Dad. We couldn't have done it alone. So many people have come alongside us to make it possible financially, physically, and spiritually.

We knew God had the right kids chosen for us in the same way he has the right family chosen for them. We just have to say yes to what Jesus asks us to do.

**Mark and Charmaine Balmer**

# Introduction

It was thrilling to hear my sister's joy when they finally made it to Ghana to meet their new children; their family was about to change forever! The dinner table became a fuller and more beautiful place to break bread!

As an aunt, my world was changed too. I had another niece and nephew to love and adore. Adoption is deeply rooted in God's heart and expresses his love and grace. As believers, we have this incredible gift of becoming a part of the family of God! I am a daughter of the king! My heavenly Father loves me and received me. I am loved. That is what adoption has done for countless children around the world.

*Lucy's Adoption Song* shares the story of the Balmer family, who welcomed Peter and Akor, who were once orphans, into the arms of loving parents, siblings, and extended family. May this book remind you of God's faithfulness to you, reader! God sees you, loves you, and welcomes you with open arms as a daughter or son of the Most High King!

Enjoy the song "Sweet Thing" by visiting www.sandeemacgregor.com; it is a tribute from my heart to all children impacted by adoption.

**Sandee Macgregor**

To all who did receive him, who believed in his name, he gave the right to become children of God. (John 1:12)

Sitting in church one day,
Lucy heard her pastor say,
"Orphans and widows need our care.
Someone needs to go out there."

Religion that is pure and undefiled before God the Father is this: to visit orphans and widows in their affliction, and to keep oneself unstained from the world. (James 1:27)

He asked the church to boldly pray,
To be Christ's hands and feet today.
She closed her eyes and bowed her head,
And prayed the prayer her pastor said,

"Bless the children in the world.
Wherever they may be,
Take them by the hand, dear Lord.
May they truly see."

Jesus said, "Let the little children come to me and do not hinder them, for to such belongs the kingdom of heaven." (Matthew 19:14)

After church, Lucy's family talked and walked
Hand in hand as Lucy thought.
She looked at Mom, "I want to know,
Will our family ever grow?"

"It's time we had a little chat
To know exactly where we're at.
Your dad and I are thrilled to say
The kids you write to many days

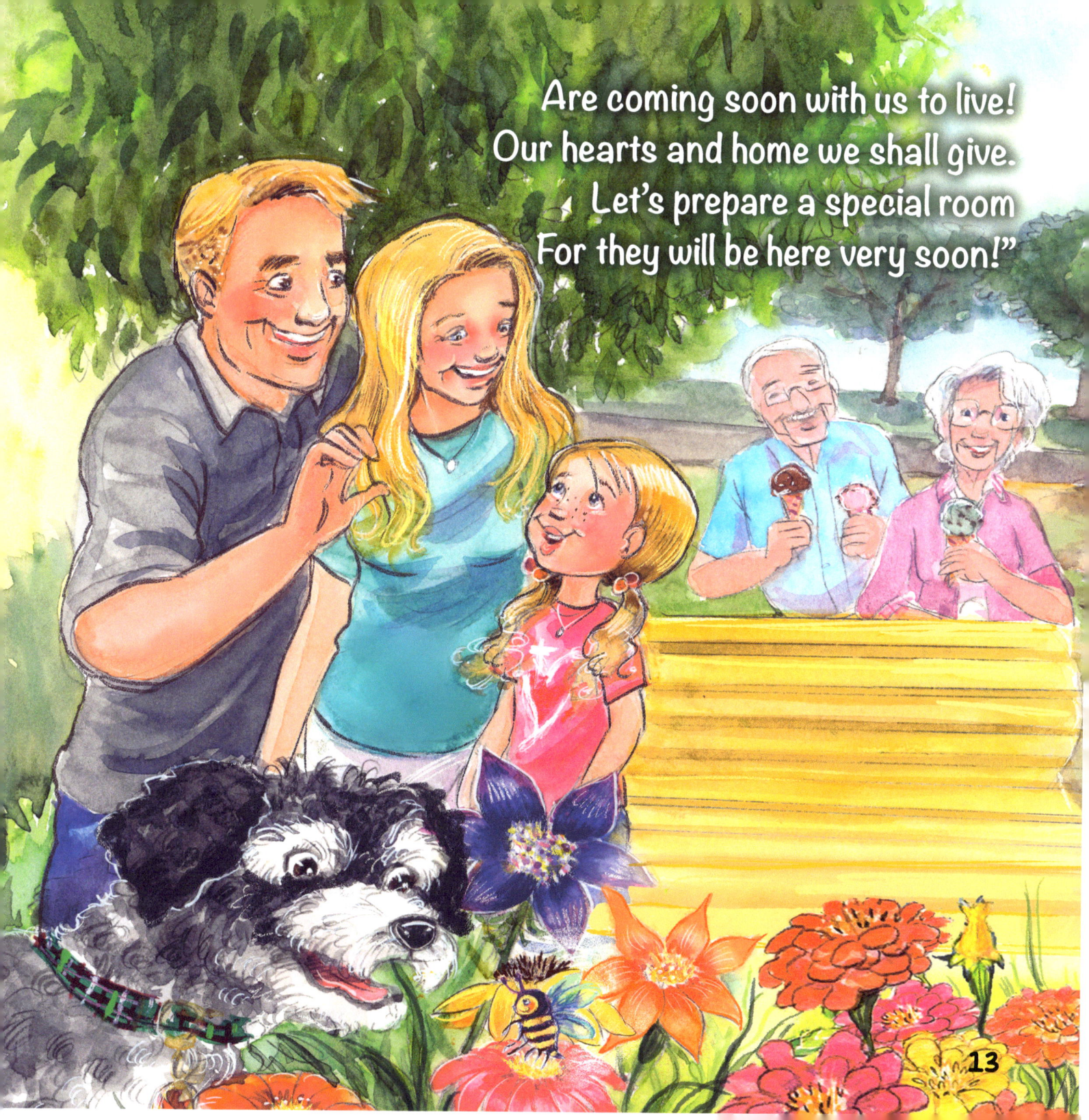

Are coming soon with us to live!
Our hearts and home we shall give.
Let's prepare a special room
For they will be here very soon!"

"I have room in my heart.
I promise I will do my part
To get ready and prepare
Comfy beds and toys to share!"

"Now let's pack and hop on a train.
Next, we have to board a plane.
We will need some clothes and toys
For all the precious girls and boys."

They arrived at a special place—
A home of love and amazing grace.
Precious children everywhere,
Singing songs they had prepared.

Sing to him, sing praises to him; tell of all his wondrous works! Glory in his holy name; let the hearts of those who seek the Lord rejoice! (Psalm 105:2–3)

All together, they sat down.
Lucy looked all around.
First came John, then came Grace.
A smile filled Lucy's face.

Lucy grabbed the little doll,
Reached inside for a brand-new ball.
She sat down with Grace on the floor;
Mom and Dad went toward the door.

They scooped up John and held him tight
Told them both, "This is just right!"
Together with hugs and tears.
"We've waited to hold you for many years!"

"As a new family, we are so excited.
To bring you home and be united."
They closed their eyes and began to pray
Words of praise and joy that day!

Because your steadfast love is better
than life, my lips will praise you.
So I will bless you as long as I live;
in your name I will lift up my hands. (Psalm 63:3–4)

The next adventure will be going home,
Never forgetting what they have known.
Africa will always be their start,
Created by God, a work of art.

Father of the fatherless and protector of widows is God in his holy habitation. God settles the solitary in a home; he leads out the prisoners to prosperity, but the rebellious dwell in a parched land. (Psalm 68:5-6)

"Whoever receives one such child in my name receives me." (Matthew 18:5)

# "Sweet Thing"
Lyrics by Cliff Cline and Kenzie Cline (commissioned by Sandee Macgregor)

Sweet thing
From when you were young
You knew rejection
Before you knew love
Sweet thing
That all will change
You have a new home
Where your heart will be safe
Oh what a privilege to care for you
Tending your wounds, I will choose to always see you

**I get to walk with you**
**Always delight in you**
**Won't always get it perfect**
**But you have my heart 'cuz you are my**
**Sweet thing**

Sweet thing
This doesn't change
The place that you came from
Will always remain
Deep in your heart
It's my prayer you'll know
You have a family wherever you go
You have a father who went to great lengths for you
I want to show you that love cause it's easy to

To hear and download the song, visit www.sandeemacgregor.com or www.kenziecline.com.

# If you liked this book, you'll like

## Can I Take It to Heaven?

Written by Sandee MacGregor

Illustrated by Kim Sponaugle

Castle Quay Books

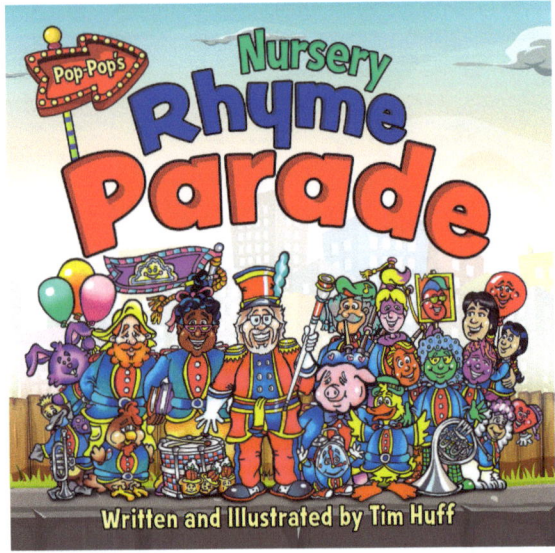
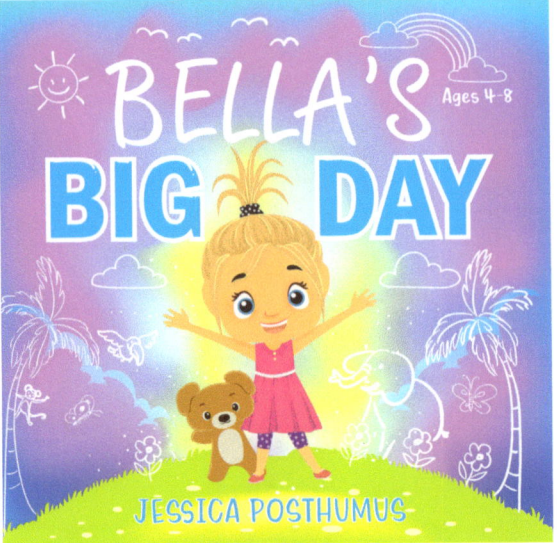
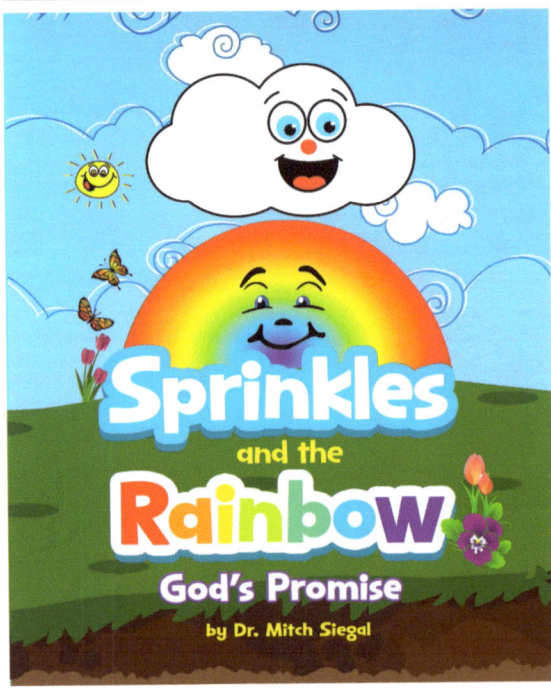
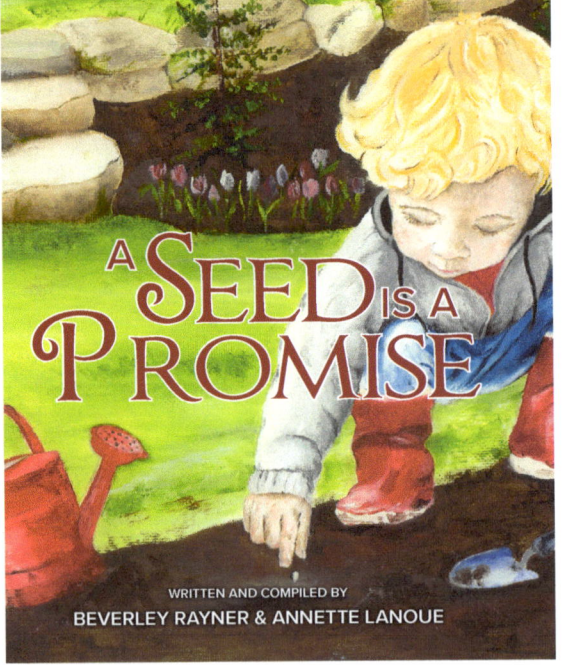

www.ingramcontent.com/pod-product-compliance
Lightning Source LLC
Chambersburg PA
CBHW040017050426
42451CB00002B/15